D0927482

IMAGES
of England

NEW FOREST

NEW FOREST
GRAMMAR SCHOOL.

(DAY AND BOARDING).

BOARDERS from **SEVEN GUINEAS** per Term
(INCLUSIVE).

DAY SCHOLARS from **ONE GUINEA** per Term.

Healthy Situation and Home Comforts.

Special attention and care given to delicate backward boys.

French, German, and Music.

PUPILS TAKEN AT ANY TIME.

ADDRESS :

THE PRINCIPAL, LYNDHURST, HANTS.

An advertisement which appeared in *Rogers' Guide to the New Forest, c.* 1900.

Contents

High School ✢ ✢

✢ ✢ for Girls,

QUEEN'S ROAD,

LYNDHURST.

Principal - - MRS. H. HOLLEY.

EXTRA CLASSES FOR VISITORS.

This advertisement appeared in Roger's *Guide to the New Forest*, *c*. 1900. Mrs Holley's husband, Henry, was a plumber.

Introduction

The curiously named 'New' Forest, tucked away in a corner of south-west Hampshire is, in fact, almost the last of the old forests which once covered England. Lying in the Hampshire basin and bordered by the Solent and Southampton Water the Forest enjoys a warm, mild climate which provides the ideal breeding ground for countless species of wildlife. The heaths and woodlands are also home to native ponies and a small, but tenacious, commoning community.

A forest, as described by John Manwood in his treatise on Forest laws, first published in 1598, is 'a certain territory of woody grounds, and pastures, privileged for wild beasts and fowls of forest, chase and warren, to rest and abide in; under the protection of the king, for his pleasure and recreation.' The ancient Forester went in fear of his life should he attempt to break the Forest law and take the king's deer. Poaching was, indeed, a serious offence, often punished by mutilation or death.

Our ancestors, though, were not only concerned with the thrills and spills of the chase. Manwood also tells us that 'the very sight and beholding of the goodly green and pleasant woods in a forest, is no less pleasant and delightful in the eyes of a prince, than the view of the wild beasts of chase; and therefore the grace of a forest is to be decked and trimmed up with store of pleasant green coverts.'

It is because those 'pleasant green coverts' still exist today that visitors come from all over the world to experience the peace and tranquillity that the ancient woodlands, the open heaths and the grassy lawns of the New Forest offer. Conservationists come to study the unique flora and fauna and the extremely rare wildlife habitats that the Forest still, against increasing odds, manages to sustain.

The Forest has attracted the great, the good and the talented of every era. Artists, writers and politicians have made their homes here, drawn irresistibly to the mix of village, rural and coastal landscape. The Forest is also, of course, a busy working environment. The administrative capital, Lyndhurst, is for many a centre for their explorations. Fascinating villages like Brockenhurst, Burley and Minstead and the market towns on the fringes, such as Fordingbridge and Lymington all have their own, very individual, appeal.

The romantic pull of the Forest is as strong as ever. Recent controversy over such matters as the siting of the Rufus Stone, or the pros and cons of becoming a National Park, only serve to reinforce the powerful sense of history felt by the inhabitants. We know that we live in a remnant of medieval England. John Moore, although only a visitor, spoke for many of us when he wrote in the 1930s:

> '...the ancientness of the Forest has a quality of darkness, there is something a little disquieting about it. The place is old in the sense that in some of its groves the shadows on the ground have not changed very much, have scarcely moved at all, since Domesday.'

A Commoners' roots are very important. The chances are that a New Forest commoning family will have tried to eke a living from the land for generations. Few locations in England, surely, in this global age, can claim such a concentration of ancient family lines. Names such as Biddlecombe, Bright, Cull, Hatch, Peckham, Purkiss, Soffe, Stride and Whitehorn, which appear over and over again in New Forest records and documents throughout the centuries, are still very much in evidence today. History records other, more flamboyant, names – Flower Archurch who became groom-keeper of Bramble Hill Walk in the late eighteenth century; Gabriel Golden, shovel maker in Minstead from the mid-1850s; and Scrope Berdmore who was vicar of All Saints, Minstead, from 1801 to 1815.

There is endless fascination with the workings and traditions of the Forest. The drifts, point-to-points, pony sales, the rights of pasture and pannage, and the Verderers Court descended from the ancient Court of Swainmote may all appear as left-overs from a bygone age, but they make the Forest what it is. The Keepers, the Agisters and most of all, the Commoners, shape and preserve all that makes the New Forest unique. I would like to dedicate this book to them.

Georgina Babey
August 2001

One
Lyndhurst – The Heart of the Forest

Lyndhurst High Street, c. 1900. The New Forest Cycle Depot is shown on the corner of Gosport Lane. The photograph was taken by John Short whose chemist shop and photographic studio were in the High Street. Established in 1829 by John's father, William, Short's pharmacy was one of the earliest shops in the High Street.

A view of Lyndhurst in the 1830s from a lithograph by T.H.S Skelton of Southampton. The well-established coaching inn, the Crown, is shown on the left. The Victorian façade that we are familiar with today appeared during the major alterations and renovations to the building that took place in the late 1890s. There was a church on the right behind the trees when the engraving was executed. A less impressive forerunner to St Michael and All Angels, it was a plain building with a squat tower. Lyndhurst was described in 1838 by Robert Mudie, thus: 'Lyndhurst is a pretty village, certainly; but the greater part of the vicinity is poor, and it looks a place out of the world; the church is in a commanding situation, but it has not much claim to attention in respect of its architecture.'

The same view of Lyndhurst, *c.* 1908, after the re-building of the Crown and the lowering of the pavement outside the church. The steps, specially built to aid passengers to mount stagecoaches, can still be seen outside the front entrance of the hotel. Around the time this photograph was taken the hotel was run by Mrs Mary Jones.

This postcard of the High Street looking east was produced by two sisters, Elizabeth and Ellen Hillyar who ran a 'fancy repository' on the south side of the High Street for more than forty years. They sold stationery, books, toys, gifts, wool and tobacco as well as post cards.

Lyndhurst High Street, c. 1905. The first shop on the left, run by George Gayler, was a draper's which doubled as a lending library. Next left was the baker's shop of Emmanuel Howells which was also 'the noted house for afternoon teas and luncheons.' The proprietor of the Fox and Hounds at this date was John Ings.

The same view in the 1960s showing the Plaza cinema on the right, now Budgen's supermarket. On this site in 1886 William Gerrard, a cabinetmaker, built a concrete edifice which became known as New Forest Hall. It was a large supper and tea rooms and boasted one of the best sprung dance floors in the south of England. Here Gerrard staged concerts, balls, all kinds of theatrical entertainments and art exhibitions each summer. It evolved into a cinema with the advent of the silent movies.

Lyndhurst High Street has always been the scene of bustling activity in the summer months. This photograph was taken in the late 1920s. The Southdown charabanc waits outside the Fox and Hounds.

High Street, Lyndhurst, *c.* 1950. The first building on the left is Lloyds Bank, still in the same position today. Lloyds re-developed the site of Short's pharmacy when John Short died in 1904.

The High Street looking west, *c.* 1880. The first house on the left, called Black House, was owned by Major Gilbert when it was demolished in 1900. Edward 'Jemmy' Gilbert, a prominent member of the New Forest Hunt, lived at Lamb's Corner, near Cadnam, now Bartley Lodge Hotel. Black House was replaced by a terrace of shops.

This view of the High Street was taken in the early 1920s. The front of the Stag Inn, on the right, was altered almost beyond recognition in 1907 but the original structure can still be seen to the rear of the building.

The east end of the High Street in the 1940s when the native ponies were still free to roam the streets. Cattle grids arrived in the New Forest in 1964, in an attempt to reduce animal deaths on the roads.

Lyndhurst Carnival on a wet day in 1911. On the north side of the street, from the left, can be seen Cheeseman's the Florist, The Volunteer Arms pub (now an estate agent), Edith Howard's stationery shop, the New Forest Hall, Adeline Payne's drapers and outfitters and, in the background, the Imperial Motor Works, opposite Gosport Lane. Adeline Payne ran an early employment agency, advertising as a 'Registry Office for Servants' with a booking fee of one shilling.

Forest Cottage Tea Gardens, *c.* 1930. Frederick Score ran the tea rooms, and also a newsagency, at the east end of the High Street.

Empress Road, Lyndhurst, *c.* 1910. The Roman Catholic church was built in 1895-96 from an endowment by Monsieur Edouard Souberbielle in memory of his wife, Marie Louise, who died while on a visit to Lyndhurst. It contains a notable marble floor and mosaics laid by Italian workers brought to England specifically for the purpose. Edouard Souberbielle lived for some time at The Cedars in Lyndhurst.

MRS. MUNNINGS,
2, HILLSIDE,
PEMBERTON ROAD, LYNDHURST.

Furnished Apartments.

PLEASANT SITUATION.

GOOD COOKING and ATTENDANCE.

TERMS MODERATE.

An advert for Mrs Munnings' establishment which appeared in a New Forest guide, *c.* 1900.

Pemberton Road, Lyndhurst, looking towards The Custards, under snow in the late 1970s.

Lyndhurst Fair on Swan Green, 9 August 1912. Judging colts for Hewitt & Gater's annual prize. The photograph was taken from an upper window of the Swan Inn. The pony sales were held on Swan Green until 1921, when the pressure of increased traffic on the A35 prompted a move to the Lyndhurst racecourse site, now the New Forest Golfcourse, between the Southampton and Romsey Roads. In the mid-1940s they moved again to their present location near the Beaulieu Road station.

St Michael & All Angels. Built in 1860, the parish church houses the famous fresco, *The Parable of the Wise and Foolish Virgins* by Frederic Leighton RA, and stained glass windows by Pre-Raphaelite artists William Morris, Burne-Jones and other members of the circle. Alice Hargreaves (*née* Lidell), the inspiration for *Alice in Wonderland*, is buried in the churchyard. She lived nearby at Cuffnells.

The King's House and church, *c.* 1915. This building, now called the Queen's House (the name changes with the gender of the ruling monarch) is the administrative headquarters of the Forestry Commission and also where the Court of Verderers is held. The building retains some medieval footings but has been extensively altered and extended over the centuries.

Jessamine Guest House, Romsey Road, now the Forest Point Hotel, *c.* 1936. The guest house was run in the 1930s by Mrs S.W. Homewood and earlier in the century by Leonard Kings. On the opposite side of the road is the old Toll Gate, called Turnpike Cottage, built in 1829 by John Shelly at a cost of £60.

Lyndhurst from the racecourse. The racecourse is now part of the New Forest Golf Club and the A337 Romsey Road, on the right, is fenced.

The Enchanted Cottage Tea Gardens in the 1950s, now operating as La Pergola restaurant, on the Southampton Road overlooking Bolton's Bench.

Cricket at Bolton's Bench in the days when there were no restrictions on cars parking on the open Forest. This change came about in the early 1970s when a system of ditches and wooden posts were introduced. Over 100 car parks and a range of campsites were established at the same time. Cricket has been played on Bolton's Bench since the early part of the nineteenth century.

Bolton's Bench is an artificial mound topped with a clump of yew and wooden seats. It commemorates the Duke of Bolton who was Lord Warden of the Forest and Master Keeper of Burley Bailiwick in the eighteenth century.

A group of young Lyndhurst men on Bolton's Bench, c. 1913. The one on the left in the straw boater is Bert Judd, the fifth from the left on the bench is W. Baker.

The Smithy at Swan Green, *c.* 1890. The smithy is the smoking single-storey building by the signpost. The smith's name was Henry Scammell and by 1895 he and his son had another site in Gosport Lane. They advertised as 'Shoeing Smiths for the two Kennels and all the neighbouring Gentry' and they used Laurel Cottage as their office. Especially interesting in this photograph is the timber strewn all over the green. In 1889 a complaint was made at the Verderers Court on the subject of the stacking and converting of timber, by steam powered cutters, on three Lyndhurst village greens. Commoners complained that their grazing rights were being infringed. When other Forest areas became affected the case, known as the Sawing Engines Case, ended in the High Court. The other thatched dwellings were, at this time, estate cottages to Northerwood House. Now, all but one are privately owned. The forge has gone.

The High Street, looking east, in the 1930s from the Romsey Road junction. The Fox and Hounds inn, on the right, has a chequered history and is said to be haunted. On New Year's Day 1867, the then landlord John Ives, was burnt to death when he fell into the fire in the bar.

Lyndhurst Station Omnibus (Bean), outside the Fox and Hounds in the High Street, c. 1932. Pink and Stretch acted as agents for the Southern Railway and ran a daily service to Lyndhurst Road station at Ashurst to meet the London trains.

The junction of Romsey Road and the High Street in the 1950s showing that the traffic congestion is not new but now, at least, there is not the added hazard of roaming stock. The offices of Gamble's the builders are on the left.

Foxlease on the Lymington Road near Goose Green has been a national training and conference centre for the Girl Guides Association since 1922. It was a gift of Mrs Archbold Saunderson 'in honour of the occasion of the marriage of our beloved President, Princess Mary.'

Lyndhurst Convalescent Cottage, Pike's Hill, *c.* 1905. The Convalescent Cottage pre-dates the Cottage Hospital (The Fenwick – see below). The two ran in conjunction for over twenty-five years. In 1911 the matron of the Convalescent Cottage above was Miss Isabel Cairnie. The house still stands and is known as Lower Bunker's Hill.

The Fenwick Cottage Hospital as it is today. It was erected in 1908 at the expense of George John Fenwick who lived at Alum Green and originally provided ten beds.

Fieldworkers near Lyndhurst. The photograph was taken from the area behind the Recreation Ground and beyond The Custards, probably from the three-acre field known as Lower Meadow. It was owned, at the time of the 1838 tithe assessment, by J. Samuel Nicholl. His near neighbour was Catherine Hinves who owned and rented land and yards round The Custards. One explanation of the derivation of its name is from the orchards of custard apples which grew there.

Steam engine transporting logs in Lyndhurst High Street during the First World War. The Steam engine is called *Queen of the South* and was owned by M. Slater of Eling. It is standing opposite the Stag Inn.

A parade of the Royal New Forest Lodge of Oddfellows at Lyndhurst, *c*. 1910.

LYNDHURST, HANTS.

TO BE

Sold by Auction,

BY

JOHN HANNEN,

At the Crown Inn, in Lyndhurst,

On **THURSDAY**, the **24th** Day of **JULY**, instant,

AT THREE O'CLOCK IN THE AFTERNOON,

A

MESSUAGE,

WITH

SHOP,

OUTBUILDINGS, and GARDEN,

SITUATE

NEAR THE CENTRE OF THE PLEASANT VILLAGE OF LYNDHURST,

AND

Now in the Occupation of Mrs. GOFFE,

AS A YEARLY TENANT.

THE PREMISES ARE FREEHOLD,

AND

Well adapted to any kind of Retail Business.

⁎⁎⁎ For further Particulars, apply (if by Letter, Post paid,) to Mr. BALDWIN, *Solicitor,* RINGWOOD.

July, 1828.

R. Galpine, Printer, Lymington.

Notice of Auction Sale of a Lyndhurst shop in July 1828. The address is not given but Mrs Goffe was the tenant. In *Pigot's Commercial Directory* of 1830 George Goffe is listed as a tailor.

Two

The Surrounding Area

Wild Ponies near Lyndhurst. The 'wild' ponies are, of course, all owned by the Commoners and managed by the Agisters. This card was posted during a heatwave in May 1961.

The Road to Forest Point, near Lyndhurst. A becalmed view of the now very busy A337 Cadnam to Lyndhurst Road.

A Forest Stream at Alum Green the tiny, ancient settlement on the outskirts of Lyndhurst. Vera Brittain bought Allum Green Cottage in May 1939. In her diary she wrote 'Heavenly cottage, heavenly spot! At least *Testament of Youth* has given me this.'

The Royal Oak pub at Bank in the 1960s. In the last decade or so the pub underwent alterations and was renamed The Oak. Bank was often visited by the young Virginia Stephen, later Woolf, as her Aunt Minna – Sarah Duckworth – lived at the house called Lane End.

Another view of the hamlet of Bank. The Huntley House guest house is shown on the left. Nearby is Annesley, built in the late 1880s by the author Mary Braddon and her husband, the publisher John Maxwell. The road leads to the isolated hamlet of Gritnam.

Emery Down, looking east, at the turn of the twentieth century. Church Cottages are on the left. Arthur Conan-Doyle stayed in Emery Down for a year from Easter 1889, while researching for his historical novel *The White Company*, which is set in the New Forest.

Emery Down, looking west, *c.* 1950. This view has changed little in the last half century. The Boultbee Cottages (almshouses) can be seen in the background. Admiral Frederick Boultbee lived at 'The Cottage' (now the vicarage) and endowed and built the church in 1864 and the almshouses in 1871. Both were designed by William Butterfield.

A cottage at Bartley. A watercolour painting by Walter Tyndale RI, RBI (1855-1943), who illustrated Horace Hutchinson's book *The New Forest* published by Methuen in 1904. A watercolourist of considerable merit, and more used to the exaggerated colour range of places such as Cairo and southern Italy, Tyndale adapted well to the more muted tones of the New Forest. He executed fifty New Forest watercolours for Hutchinson's book and seventy-five for A & C Black's *Wessex*, mostly of Dorset, published in 1906. Tyndale's direct line descendants, his grand-daughter Diana Daniell and great-grand-daughter Judith Warbey, an engraver, live in Ringwood.

Bartley post office and stores in the early part of the twentieth century from Brockishill Road. The grocer and sub-postmistress, at this time, was Elizabeth J. Weetman. Built in 1905 it is still known by some as Weetman's Corner.

Bartley church, *c.* 1945. Recently, the locally renowned 'tin church', having fallen into disuse, was threatened with demolition. As a result of pressure from local residents it was rebuilt in the original style and is now a thriving community hall.

Cadnam Village, *c.* 1913. The Sir John Barleycorn pub is in the left foreground, and clearly shows the old Romsey Road. In the right foreground is the road to Ringwood. The photograph is by Willsteed of Southampton, a prolific photographer of New Forest villages in the early part of the twentieth century.

Twin Oaks, Cadnam, *c.* 1938. The oaks are still standing but the thatched wooden cottage, advertising Toogoods Seeds, Southampton, has been demolished.

The Inn Sign, Trusty Servant, Minstead. The original of the sign is a sixteenth-century painting which hangs in Winchester College and depicts 'the perfect servant' – a padlocked mouth, unable to tell his masters' secrets, the patience of an ass and the swift feet of the deer. In the top left hand corner is the motto of Winchester College 'Manners Makyth Man'.

A Trusty Servant's portrait would you see,
This Emblematic Figure well survey;
The Porker's Snout not nice in diet shews;
The Padloch Shut no secrets he'll disclose.
Patient the Ass his Master's Wrath will bear;
Swiftness in errand the Stagg's Feet declare;
Loaded his Left Hand apt to labour saith;
The Vest his neatness; Open Hand his faith;
Girt with his Sword his Shield upon his arm;
Himself and master he'll protect from harm.

Outside the Trusty Servant, in the middle of the village green, is a horse chestnut tree surrounded by an oak bench. This photograph was taken soon after the tree was planted in honour of the Silver Jubilee of King George V and Queen Mary in 1935. The proprietor of the inn at this time was Francis Wolfe.

All Saints, Minstead. The church shows some evidence of Norman architecture and it houses an unusual triple-decker pulpit, two galleries and family pews for the gentry with their own fireplace. During recent renovations to the church a copy of the 1838 tithe map was found. Arthur Conan-Doyle is buried in the churchyard. He had a home nearby at Bignell Wood.

Although this photograph is captioned 'Wayside Cottage, Lyndhurst' it is, in fact, Ivy Cottage in Minstead opposite Seaman's Lane junction.

Rufus Stone, Canterton Glen, *c.* 1905. The stone, now encased in iron, marks the spot where, according to tradition, King William Rufus fell while hunting in the Forest on 2 August 1100.

An engraving of the Rufus Stone by T.P. Andrews which appeared in *Gentleman Magazine*, September 1786, forty years after it was first erected by John, Lord Delaware.

Compton Arms Hotel, Stoney Cross. The Compton Arms was named for the Compton family who were Lords of the Manor of Minstead for four hundred years. The hotel offered rest to the traveller for over a hundred years. It is now a travel lodge. In 1934, Joan Begbie writing in her book *Walking in the New Forest*, says of it: 'the airy Compton Arms, with such luxuries as running water in nearly every bedroom, and a kindly management which packs up lunches for the walker... There are hacks and hunters to be had from the hotel stables, and loose boxes for your own beasts should you bring them along... The terms are from five guineas a week *en pension*.'

Part View Garden, Compton Arms Hotel
Stoney Cross, Near Lyndhurst, Hants

Dick Turpin's Cottage, Stoney Cross. 'Just over the way' from the Compton Arms, this guesthouse and tea rooms took visitors from two to thtee guineas a week in the 1930s. Described by Begbie as: 'a tiny place run by cheerful people who assure us that they thoroughly understand the needs of the walker.' The cheerful people were the Iles family.

Maypole dancing outside the Monkey Tree Hotel, Ashurst, 1948/49. The piano accordion is played by Brian Godwin. The Monkey Tree was run at this time by W.M. Haslam. It was bought, in 1954, by Michael Leonard whose father Reginald ran the Angry Cheese tea rooms and restaurant on the opposite side of the road. Michael renamed the Monkey Tree the Happy Cheese and, as such, it gained a reputation for excellent, if expensive, cuisine. On 15 May 1976 the Happy Cheese was destroyed by fire. Two and a half years passed before it was rebuilt, on a much smaller scale, and re-opened for business. It never regained its former reputation for *haute cuisine* and is today a pleasant family pub.

A rare photograph of Woodlands Road, Ashurst, showing the area around the junction with Fletchwood Lane and opposite Costicles Inclosure, c. 1937. Most of these houses were built after the First World War by the newly affluent middle classes.

Southampton Road, Ashurst in the 1930s. On the left is Ashurst Motor Works which was opened by Alfred Nicholls in the early 1920s. A garage is still on the site today.

Chalet Café Ashurst, c. 1950. This was a popular stopping-off spot in The Terrace at Ashurst in the 1940s and '50s. It was destroyed by fire in the mid-1960s and was not rebuilt. Since then the site has been a second-hand car sales yard.

New Forest Hotel, Ashurst, c. 1910. The hotel, situated by the railway station, ran a regular horse-bus (and later motor-bus) service to Lyndhurst during the heyday of train travel.

THE "ROSE & CROWN,"

Family & Commercial Hotel,

BROCKENHURST, Hants.

E. INGS, Proprietress.

BROCKENHURST is a convenient centre, being within 4 miles of Lyndhurst and 5 miles of Lymington ; and is also within easy distance of the principal places of interest in the New Forest. The Woodland Scenery in the neighbourhood is exceptionally fine.

BRAKES AND CARRIAGES for drives to Lyndhurst, Bolderwood, Mark Ash, Rufus' Stone, and Queen's Bower, on the shortest notice, with experienced Drivers that know the Forest.

This old-established Hotel is well suited for Gentlemen and Families.

PRIVATE SITTING ROOMS OR SUITES if necessary can be had on application.

First-class Stabling for Hunters if required.

An advert for the Rose & Crown Hotel as it appeared in the fifth edition of W.H. Roger's *Guide to the New Forest* from around 1900, when it was run by Eleanor Ings.

Brockenhurst Carnival, in aid of the Brockenhurst Schools Enlargement Fund, 1914. The procession is outside the Rose and Crown Hotel in Lyndhurst Road. The building on the left is the Baptist chapel, now a private residence. The parade and band can be seen behind the collector, in white, on the left. The photograph is by Frederick Davis who had a business in Lyndhurst High Street with a second branch at Hounsdown.

The Watersplash, Brookley Road, Brockenhurst, in the late 1950s looking towards Little Brookley in the Rhinefield Road.

Three
Forest at Work

'Mr Bright's Outfit.' Mr Bright and companion extracting timber with a steam-powered sawmill in Bolderwood, February 1934. Mr Edward Bright lived at Pear Tree Farm, Emery Down.

Queen's Mead Bridge, which crosses Highland Water a little to the north of Queen's Bower near Brockenhurst, was first built in 1843 by John Broad. When, in the winter of 1928, the bridge gave way and was beyond repair, work on a new bridge began. The workers were George (surname unknown), Harry Tucker who lived at Rhinefield Cottage and Bill and Jim (Jimmer) Gates.

George with the Rammer. The building of the new bridge was captured in watercolour by Alice Hindson, one of four sisters who lived at Deerleap, Wilverley Road, Brockenhurst. She later had her paintings, with accompanying calligraphic text, bound in leather and it has become a unique record of the building of a New Forest bridge.

The twenty-first day – fitting the handrails. The fine weather holds and the bridge nears completion.

Carting away the timber. Alice and her sister Blanche died in the 1980s. The other two sisters, one of whom became Mrs Vesey-Fitzgerald, then lived at Forest Oaks, The Rise, Brockenhurst.

Disc ploughing on the Forest during the Second World War, March 1944. The Second World War left an indelible mark on the Forest landscape. Large areas were given over to the military to form airfields, bombing ranges, training and firing zones, as well as sawing sites and prisoner-of-war camps. The heath was covered with barbed wire and live explosives and, as this photograph shows, areas previously used for stock grazing were given over to cultivation.

The location is probably Whitefield Moor and the driver of the plough is Mr W. Ingram. The War Department was unwilling to give up its new-found training ground after the war but was gradually forced to give way to local and national pressure. Even so, it was well into the 1950s before the Forest returned to anything approaching pre-war normality.

Rhinefield Forest Nursery, July 1947. Lumberjills, employed by the Forestry Commission, taking a break. From left to right: Margaret Dunkinson, Rose Cutler (partly screened by Margaret Bessant), Ivy Smith, Joyce Curtis, Millie Perkins, Lottie Bowden and Barbara Carter.

Felling an oak in Setthorns Inclosure, late 1941. Fred Pardey of Purley Cottage, Chapel Lane, Sway is on the left and his brother, Bill Pardey, of Central Cottage, Chapel Lane, Sway, on the right.

The Pardey brothers, after the preparation work with axes, take to a crosscut saw, and then watch their giant fall.

The Pardey brothers clearing the smaller branches from the felled oak.

Log-rolling in Beachern Wood. Fred Pardey is in the white shirt and the young Eddie Gulliver is holding the horse. The white horse is called Blossom and the one harnessed to the cart is Whitefoot.

Number of the Claim.	Name and Abode of the Claimant.		Land or Tenements in respect of which he Claims.	
	Claimant.	Agent.	Property.	Quantity.
				A. R. P.
760	Sarah Phelps, Picket Post	— —	Dwelling-house used as a house, out-houses, land, and premises, called Picket Post	4 0 0
			House, outhouses, garden, and orchard adjoining	1 0 0
			Dwelling-house, outhouses, with garden and premises, called Dilamgerbendi Villa, all situate about 200 yards to the west of Picket Post	1 0 0
761	William Biel, St. Leonard's Beaulieu	James Brown, St. Thomas-street, Lymington	3 houses and land at Rowdown, near Fawley	8 0 0
762	Nancy Ryder Soffe, Spring Cottage, Fawley	— —	2 houses, gardens, orchard, land, and premises, called Arnolds and Perrys, at Rowdown	8 0 0
763	Reverend Augustus Hewitt, Warwick William Hughes Hughes, senr. and William Hughes Hughes, junr. of Brunswick-square, London, and Jonathan Muckleston Key, Fordingbridge	— —	2 tenements, stable, garden, orchard, and premises, at Rookham Bottom, near Fordingbridge	about 1 0 0
764	Frances Prewett, Godshill, near Fordingbridge	Hy. Tremenheere Johns, Ringwood	Tenement, stable, outhouses, yard, garden, and premises, at Rookham bottom	0 1 30
765	William Angel, Woodgreen	— —	House and orchard, Woodgreen	1 0 0
766	George Best, Godshill	— —	House and orchard, Woodgreen	1 0 0
767	William Chubb, Godshill	— —	Land extra-parochial, Woodgreen	2 0 0
768	William Briant, Godshill	— —	Land extra-parochial, Woodgreen	2 0 0
769	William Chalk, Woodfall's Hill, Downton	William Stead, Romsey, Hants	A double dwelling-house, orchard, gardens, and premises, at Woodgreen, adjoining the parish of Breamore	0 3 0
770	William Dyer, Caterham, Surrey	John Woodlands, Downton, Wilts	Woodgreen	1 2 0
771	Richard Downer, Woodgreen	— —	Land at Woodgreen	2 0 0
			Land at Woodgreen under Frederic Breton	1 0 0
772	Lydia Edsall, Marchwood	Nathaniel Philpot, Marshwood	Cottage, garden, and orchard at Woodgreen	0 2 0
773	Henry Harrington, Woodgreen	— —	House and orchards at Woodgreen	2 0 0
774	William Mowland, Woodgreen, near Breamore	— —	Orchard, garden, and premises at Woodgreen	3 0 0
775	James Newham, Nunton, Wilts	— —	House, out-buildings, garden, orchard, and land at Woodgreen	1 1 0
776	Humphrey Pinhorn, Fordingbridge	— —	6 cottages, garden, orchards, and premises at Woodgreen	3 0 0
777	William Robson and Thomas Worsfold, of Wilton, as devisees in fee under the will of George Wort, deceased.	Richard Nightingale, Lyndhurst	House, garden, orchard and premises at Woodgreen	1 1 0
778	James Stride, Woodgreen	— —	House and land	3 0 0
779	James Stride, Woodgreen	— —	Orchard and garden, at Woodgreen	3 0 0
780	William Trim, Woodgreen	— —	House and orchard, at Woodgreen	0 3 0
781	Frances Witt, Woodgreen	— —	Five cottages, gardens, orchards, and land, at Woodgreen	4 0 0
782	George White, Woodgreen	— —	House and land at Woodgreen	1 3 0
783	John Witt, Bridford	George Witt, Woodgreen	House, garden, orchard, land, and premises at Woodgreen	2 0 0
784	George Witt, Woodgreen	— —	House, orchard, garden, and premises at Woodgreen	1 0 0

A typical page from the 1852 *Abstract of Claims*. Hundreds of properties in and around the New Forest are or were subject to claim one or more of the Forest rights of pasture, sheep, fuelwood, mast (pigs at pannage), and the now obsolete rights of marl (for fertilizer) and turbary (a peat-like substance for

ABSTRACT OF CLAIMS.

The Subject-matter of the Claim.

Common of Pasture.	Common of Pannage.	Common of Turbary.	Common of Estovers.		Other Rights Claimed.
For all cattle and other beasts, other than sheep, and goats, and swine, and geese	For swine	Turbary and heath	—	—	To dig, cut, and take gravel, sand, marl, fern, peat, furze, and water
For all cattle except sheep and goats	In pannage time	Turbary and heath	—	—	Furze, and to dig and carry away marl
For all commonable cattle, except sheep	For all hogs	Turbary 4000, and heath	—	—	Fern and furze
For all cattle, except sheep	For all hogs	Turf and heath	—	—	Fern and furze
For 2 horned cattle, 1 horse, and 5 pigs	—	—	3000 turves and heath	—	—	3 loads of fern with furze, 1000 peat
For 2 cows, 1 horse	—	—	Turbary, 2 loads	—	—	Fern, 2 loads
For 2 cows	—	—	Turbary	—	—	
For 1 cow	—	—	Turbary, 2 loads	—	—	Fern, 2 loads
For 1 cow	—	—	Turbary, 2 loads	—	—	Fern, 2 loads
For all commonable cattle, except sheep	For all hogs	Turf and heath			
Pasturage for 3 cows	—	—	Turf for 2 cottages	—	—	Fern for 2 cows
For 1 cow	—	—	Turbary, 2 loads			
For 1 head of cattle	For all hogs	4 loads of turf and heath	—	—	Fern and furze
To graze cattle	—	—	Turbary			
For all commonable cattle, except sheep	For all hogs	2000 turves and heath	—	—	Fern and furze
For all commonable cattle, except sheep	For all hogs	Turf and heath	—	—	Fern and furze
For all cattle and commonable animals (except sheep), and goats	For swine	Turbary, turf, and heath	—	—	To dig, cut, and take gravel, land, marl, clay, and water and furze
For 2 head of cattle	For four hogs	2000 turves or peat			
The run for 2 head of cattle	—	—	Turf	—	—	Fern
For all commonable cattle, except sheep	For all hogs	2000 turves and heath	—	—	Fern and furze
For one head of cattle and 6 hogs	For all hogs	2000 turves and heath	—	—	Fern and furze
For all commonable cattle, except sheep	For all hogs	Turbary, 10 loads and heath	—	—	Fern and furze
To graze cattle	—	—	Turbary			
For all commonable cattle, except sheep	For all hogs	2000 turves annually and heath	—	—	Fern and furze
For all commonable cattle, except sheep	For all hogs	Turbary 2000, and heath	—	—	Fern and furze

burning). Registers and abstracts of these claims, which detail the names of all the properties and the Commoners claiming their rights to 'farm' the Forest, were published in the eighteenth and nineteenth centuries and give a unique social record of the Forest's Commoning heritage.

Fern gatherers, New Forest. One of the two 'Forest harvests' (the other being holly) fern was cut in the autumn and used as animal bedding.

CUTTING BRACKEN AT STONEY CROSS
THE NEW FOREST

This print, *Cutting Bracken at Stoney Cross*, is by living New Forest artist Barry Peckham. Heywood Sumner, in his *Book of Gorley* published in 1910, describes ferning: 'The fern is cut by the Forest men and carried by the buyers. A load of fern delivered here costs 8s, and the loads are full measure, twelve feet high from the ground ... and then the moving brown stacks creak slowly homeward along the rutty Forest tracks, to supply litter for the small farmers...'

Charcoal making was an important New Forest industry for many centuries. The photograph shows a charcoal burner's hut, common in the nineteenth century. The traditional method of charcoal making consisted of a carefully constructed dome of cord wood, thinner towards the outside, and covered with hay or bed fuzzing and then sealed with earth to exclude the air. A burn took several days and the pit needed constant surveillance. The charcoal burners, known as colliers, would stay at one site for as long as the wood lasted and they lived in huts such as this one, made from poles lashed together at the top and covered in turf for warmth and weatherproofing.

Modern charcoal making, 1973. Laurie Gardner of Minstead (left), Stuart Smith, head forester on the Lockerley Estate near Romsey (middle) and John Carter of Lyndhurst (right), examine the cord wood in preparation for a kiln burn.

Laurie and John lay the cord wood – branches of oak and beech – in horizontal layers in the lower half of the kiln.

The wood must smoulder slowly, controlled by draught holes in the base. If the fire is allowed to become too fierce a pile of ash is all that will remain.

The result of many weeks work – ten tons of stacked charcoal – will be used in copper smelting, gunpowder production and the manufacture of man-made fibres. It is also used in water-filter beds, for artists' pencils and, of course, barbecues.

Preparing for the drift, Markway, 1991. Agisters, and other skilled riders, gather at points all over the Forest every autumn to round-up the ponies.

The riders are capable of gauging every nuance in the temperament of the feral ponies, anticipating their movements, and leading them, skilfully, to the waiting pound.

Drift on Beaulieu Heath, East of Crabhat, 1991. On the right of the photograph is Ralph Hayward. A lifetime Commoner from Fawley, Ralph has ridden in drifts and point-to-points for decades. He is almost certain to hold the record for the shortest term as a Verderer. He was co-opted for four days in November 2000 in recognition of his life-long service to the Forest.

Once 'caught-in' any ponies not destined for the sales will be tail-marked, wormed and hot branded, and the Agisters will ascertain the amount of marking fees that are due from their Commoner owners.

An old Forester collecting autumn leaves with his donkey cart. H.M. Livens, in his book *Nomansland*, published in 1910, says: 'With the fall of the beech and oak leaves comes the time of leaf-gathering. These ... are raked up and carted home by the villagers, to serve first as litter, and afterwards as food for the land.'

Bramshaw Forge, Stocks Cross, *c.* 1920. Arthur Cooper is on the far left and his son Eli is shoeing. The smithy at Bramshaw was operational from at least the end of the eighteenth century until its closure in 1997. It was run by the Cooper family from the middle of the nineteenth century until 1942. It is now a private house.

Thomas White, 1781-1850. White was Steward to the Lord Warden of the New Forest from 1817 until his death. His term of office was not without intrigue. He survived, although not unscathed, an enquiry into 'misdeeds and misappropriations' within the Forest. He lived in King's House (now Queen's House), Lyndhurst and was paid an annual salary of £110. He is buried in Lyndhurst churchyard.

A unique view of the Verderer's Court from the sketchbook of Eleanor White, c. 1830. Eleanor was the daughter of Thomas White. She grew up in King's House and was married to Robert Harfield, at Lyndhurst church in 1847. The Verderer's Court, one of the most ancient in the country, still meets regularly to hear presentments and make decisions on Forest concerns.

Appletree Court, *c.* 1925. Since 1948, Appletree Court has been home to the New Forest District Council. The house was built by Edward Penton in 1919, on land that was once part of the Glasshayes estate (now Lyndhurst Park Hotel). Designed by the architect Kitchin, who also worked on renovations in Winchester Cathedral, it had nineteen bedrooms and an impressive, broad corridor running the length of the house.

Princess Anne talking to Head Agister Brian Ingram at the New Forest Show, July 2000. From left to right: Agister Andrew Napthine, Agister Jonathan Gerrelli, the Princess Royal, Head Agister Brian Ingram, and Official Verderer Maldwin Drummond.

The New Forest Show, 1965. Presentation of awards by the president's wife. The New Forest and Hampshire County Show, now a massive three-day event, draws huge crowds from all over the country.

Lord Montagu of Beaulieu, in an exhibit from his Motor Museum, escorts the Dairy Queen, New Forest Show, 1965. Since 1955 the show has been held at New Park, Brockenhurst.

A trade stand at the New Forest Show, 1965. One of the men between the tractors is Wilf Waterman. The first ever live stock show, the forerunner of the present day event, was held at Bartley Cross, near Cadnam in the summer of 1920.

A competitor in the jumping classes of the New Forest Show arena events, 1965.

Four
The Forest Character

Agister Gerald Forward (1898-1980), centre, with two companions outside the Royal Oak, Fritham. A Commoner for most of his life, Forward also served as an Agister for twenty-five years, and in 1959 became an elected Verderer. The knowledge and expertise that he brought to the Forest remains unsurpassed.

William Gilpin, Vicar of Boldre from 1777-1804. Gilpin was a social and educational reformer as well as a writer and artist. Gilpin did not take up his living at Boldre until he was in his fifties but his impact on the Forest was immediate and lasting.

Gilpin's home, The Vicarage, *c.* 1914, Here he wrote and illustrated his famous work *Remarks on Forest Scenery*, which was first published in 1791.

Gilpin's School, at Pilley, Boldre, from his own drawing 1791. Finding his parishioners an unruly and uneducated band, Gilpin devoted his life at Boldre to improving their lot. He built, at his own expense, a Poor House and a Model Free School.

Gilpin's School, now a private residence, as it was in 1971. There is still a school dedicated to his name in Boldre. William Gilpin died aged eighty and is buried in Boldre churchyard.

Mr Mudge of Brookley Farm Manor (now the Watersplash Hotel in The Rise), Brockenhurst, 1873. Richard Mudge was, according to his neighbour Lady Bowden Smith, writing in her memoirs, 'a quaint and familiar sight as he rode about on his stout white cob'.

'A Visit from Queen Bess', part of the New Forest Pageant, 1 and 2 June 1921. Organized by Brockenhurst Women's Institute, the pageant presented historical scenes connected with the Forest. It took place in Manor Park and was visited by a great crowd from as far away as Bournemouth. The whole village played some part in the entertainment.

Gilbert Smith (1906-85), Forest keeper. Born at Holly Hatch Cottage, his father and grandfather were Forest Keepers, and when his father retired from Ashurst beat in 1950, Gilbert took over. Gilbert saw great changes in Forest management in his life as a Forester, witnessing, to his great sorrow, the devastating fellings in the ancient and ornamental woodlands. He recognized that the consequent increase in softwoods led to the loss of bird and wild flower habitats. His book *New Forest Recollections* was published posthumously. He is buried in Lyndhurst Cemetery. On his gravestone are the words: 'The Heart of the Forest – Now in the Forest's Heart'.

Colonel Alexander and Mabel Macleay who lived at Glasshayes (on the site of the present day Lyndhurst Park Hotel) from around 1872 to 1895.

Glasshayes, when the Macleays were in residence, c. 1880. By 1899 Glasshayes had become The Grand Hotel and was run by Tilley & Courtenay. Later the Macleays lived at Okefield, Bolton's Bench.

The Grand Hotel, *c.* 1938. Glasshayes in another of its guises. It is now called the Lyndhurst Park Hotel.

'Old Tame'. Farmer, gardener and lay preacher Henry Tame lived at Bolderwood. A strong character, he was well known in the Forest for his eccentric ways and his longevity. When he was 100 years old he had a new pair of boots made for him but complained to the bootmaker that they were too thin and wouldn't last. His gravestone records that he died on 2 February 1900, aged 103 years and 11 months. He is buried in the Baptist churchyard in Lyndhurst. The drawing is by Heywood Sumner.

H·S.

Old Tame

Perhaps the most famous of all the Forest characters is the snakecatcher, Harry 'Brusher' Mills (1840-1905). Brusher caught snakes which he sold to London Zoo for one shilling each. His bizarre occupation, coupled with his colourful character, have ensured him a strong place in the history of the Forest. This oil portrait of Brusher, painted by Leonard Skeats around 1895, is probably the only painting of him ever executed while he was alive.

For nearly twenty years Brusher Mills lived the life of a hermit in a disused charcoal burner's hut near Brockenhurst. One of his favourite haunts was the nearby Railway Inn where his body was found in an outhouse on 1 July 1905. His way of life had weakened his chest and heart. He is buried in Brockenhurst churchyard. The Railway Inn was renamed The Snakecatcher in recent times.

Boa Constrictor caught in the New Forest, 24 August, 1904. The snake, an escaped pet, was captured one and a half miles from Emery Down by Edward Sims, Keeper at Holidays Hill which is now the home of the New Forest Reptile Centre.

Not a modern-day snakecatcher but Peter Frost, chairman of the New Forest Association for seventeen years and now a Verderer. Peter is a tireless worker for the cause of the conservation of the Forest. While on a day's walk with friends, in 1991, he found a harmless grass snake near Brockenhurst. His companions did not, apparently, share his enthusiasm for reptiles!

Three generations of the Hayter family of Pennington in 1901. James Hayter senior (centre), a bricklayer by profession, served as parish clerk and sexton for sixty years. By a peculiar coincidence he entered this office, was married and died, aged eighty-six, all on Christmas Day. His son Edward (probably seen here on the left) was a coach trimmer.

Charlie Poulton, eel-trap maker of Woodgreen, c. 1939. Made of seasoned hazel rods, the traps, about 3ft long, were carefully woven with a narrow opening at one end. The traps held about 3lb of small eels and were used in the Avon watermeadows. Charlie still made the traps in his nineties not wanting to 'bide een doors.'

Frank Whittington (1876-1973) at work in his Brockenhurst toy factory. Frank and his wife, the painter and commercial artist Marjorie Hood, came to Brockenhurst after the First World War and set up a business producing hand carved wooden toys. By 1922 the toys were so popular that the factory employed sixteen men and women.

This advert appeared in Russell's *Guide to the New Forest*, 1936. As well as New Forest animals, Whittingtons specialized in Noah's Arks, farmyard figures and stagecoaches. They were bought by Harrods, Selfridges and other major London stores. The factory closed at the outbreak of the Second World War because of difficulties in obtaining supplies.

THE FOREST TOYS
F. H. Whittington

BROCKENHURST   Telephone : 54

You are invited to visit the Workshops. Hand Carved and painted animals of all kinds, true to life and in correct proportion.   Prices from 6d. to 5/- each.

ILLUSTRATED CATALOGUE POST FREE

Heywood Sumner (1853-1940), in his study at Cuckoo Hill, South Gorley. One of the forerunners of the Arts and Crafts movement, Sumner was a skilled artist, writer and archaeologist. He made a unique contribution to the knowledge and understanding of archaeological sites in the Forest.

Cuckoo Hill, South Gorley. The house that Sumner built for his family in the early part of the twentieth century and the building of which he chronicled in *The Book of Gorley* first published in 1910. The house, shown below in 1993, is now a care home for the elderly.

Gypsy hawker chair mender in the New Forest, c. 1890. New Forest gypsies were a common sight on the open Forest until 1926 when they were forced into compounds and from there into council houses. They lived traditionally in bender tents or tans – tarpaulin stretched over bent hazel rods. A hardy and resourceful people, they earned their living by hawking their wares or offering services. This photograph is by John Short of Lyndhurst.

Head Keeper Ted Smith with the heads of two red deer stags that died in combat, their antlers locked together. Bucks (male fallow and roe) and stags (red) will fight desperately in the autumn rutting season.

Stags fighting. This illustration is from William Gilpin's *Remarks on Forest Scenery*, 1791. Two more examples of interlocking antlers can be found in the Verderer's Court, one of roe and one fallow.

The New Forest artist, Frederick Golden Short (1863-1936) in his Lyndhurst studio. Son of the photographers John and Elizabeth Short, Frederick attended Southampton Art School and, later, earned his living selling his timeless New Forest landscapes.

Autumn from Bramble Hill by Frederick Golden Short. Frederick was only eighteen when this, and several other of his drawings, were used in F.G. Heath's New Forest book *Autumnal Leaves*, published in 1881.

Gerald Lascelles by Sir Leslie Ward (alias 'Spy') as he appeared in the magazine *Vanity Fair* on 23 September 1897. Lascelles was Deputy Surveyor of the New Forest from 1880 until his retirement in 1914. His memoirs of this time, *Thirty-Five Years in the New Forest*, were published the following year.

The Broad family at Amberwood, *c.* 1906. Woodman Albert Broad lived at Amberwood Cottage with his wife Anna Maria, son and two daughters. From left to right: Daisy, Albert, Ellen, Anna Maria, and Albert Jnr.

Anna Maria and Ellen Broad in the garden of Amberwood Cottage, *c.* 1906. Topiary was once a popular occupation in Forest cottage gardens. Amberwood Cottage was wrecked by activity from the adjacent Ashley Walk Bombing Range in the Second World War.

John Wise, New Forest author, 27 September 1879. The only known portrait of the author of the standard work *The New Forest: its History and Scenery* (1863), is this drawing by his young friend and colleague, the illustrator Walter Crane.

One of Walter Crane's illustrations from *The New Forest*, in the chapter dealing with Wise's exploration of the Roman and Romano-British pottery sites. Crane was only sixteen years of age when he was commissioned to accompany John Wise on his walking tour of the Forest to research the book.

Five
Trade and Enterprise

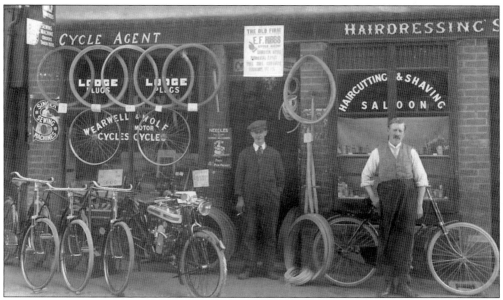

Edward Frank Hibbs operated as a cycle and motorcycle agency in Brookley Road, Brockenhurst in the 1920s. Frank Hibbs is shown standing in the doorway. Hibbs later had another outlet in Romsey Road, Lyndhurst. The Brockenhurst shop was taken over by Frank Jenvey.

Hendy Engineering Works displaying their wares at a show, probably the forerunner of the New Forest County Show at Cuffnells Park, Lyndhurst in the 1940s. Hendy's were automobile and agriculture engineers specialising in Ford cars and Fordson tractors.

Frank Chalk's Fish and Game shop, c. 1910. Chalk's, also a greengrocers, operated in Brookley Road, Brockenhurst for several decades.

Dear's of Brockenhurst, now an estate agency next to the Foresters Arms, around 1914. Mr Dear is standing behind the woman on the left in the photograph. The first gentleman on the right, nearest to the window, is Mr Albert Baker who became the owner of Dear's after Mr Alfred Gosling.

G. Elliott & Son, tailors and outfitters, in Brookley Road, Brockenhurst (next to the post office) in the 1930s.

The Island Shop adjacent to Brockenhurst station in the 1920s when it operated as a barber and tobacconist. Dear's shop, still operating as a butcher's, can be seen in the background.

The back of the Island Shop, c. 1920. It stands on the site of the master smithy. The smith before the Great War was Mr T. Street who later opened a hardware shop in Brookley Road. The Morant Arms in the background is named in honour of the Lords of the Manor.

Mr and Mrs Street were married at Brockenhurst Parish church on 4 August 1902. Mr Street, born in Kent, came to Brockenhurst as a blacksmith during the Boer War. He was a member of the Brockenhurst Parish Council for many years. Mr and Mrs Street (*née* Povey) are photographed here, on their Golden Wedding anniversary in 1952. They opened their ironmonger's store in Brookley Road in 1927 and it is still going strong today.

Mrs Rosina Price's drapery and boot store, Manchester Road, Sway in the 1930s. The store was built onto a cob cottage. It was demolished in 1998.

Miss Pardey's grocery shop, Chapel Lane, Sway. Seen here are Miss Florence (Fanny) and Lou Pardey.

Strange's of Lyndhurst, *c.* 1980. One of the oldest established businesses in the New Forest, Robert Strange was listed as a butcher in Lyndhurst in *Pigot's Trade Directory* of 1844. Strange's were famous all over the south for their venison sausages.

J.W. Martin, chemist, Brookley Road, Brockenhurst. John William Martin is listed as a chemist in *Kellys' Directories* of the 1920s. He was also a keen photographer.

The chemist shop, *c.* 1945. The shop was now being run by John's son Ken. Outside the shop is Mrs Martin, her daughter Jane and assorted members of the New Forest Hounds.

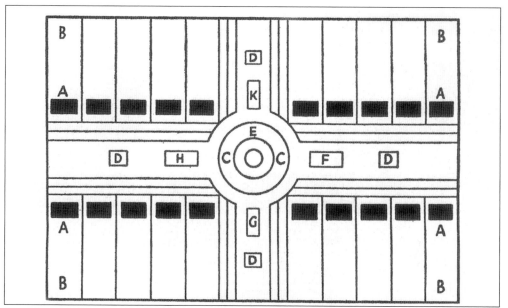

Daniel Defoe, in 1722, proposed a naive plan to re-populate what he described as one of the 'wast and wild' spaces of the Forest. Defoe's proposal was to offer twenty refugee families £200 and 200 acres of land each, set on a rigid grid-plan, with a central 'model town'. Defoe's idea was never taken seriously.

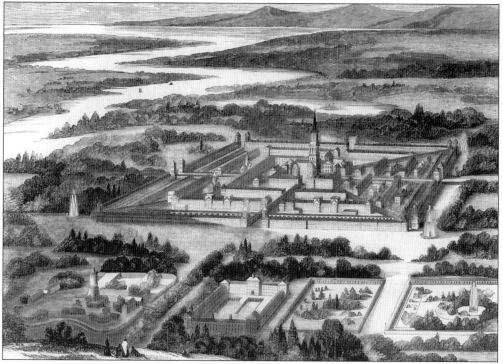

Defoe's failure did not stop James Buckingham coming up with another 'model town plan' in 1849. The plan for his proposed town, to be called Victoria, shows its location on the Beaulieu River with the Isle of Wight in the background.

Buckler's Hard, a tiny hamlet two and a half miles from Beaulieu on the west bank of the Beaulieu River, played an important part in Britain's naval history for two centuries. In 1743 the firm of Wyatt & Co., set up a shipbuilding business here, encouraged by John, the second Duke of Montagu.

The oak-built ships launched from Buckler's Hard, under the auspices of master-builder Henry Adams, took part in nearly every important battle during the Napoleonic Wars, including the Battle of Trafalgar. In the First World War motor launches were built here and wooden minesweepers fitted out in the Second World War. Today there is a Maritime Museum at Buckler's Hard and the Master Builder's House is a hotel and restaurant. The illustration is from Percival Lewis's work on the New Forest published in 1811.

Six

Village Life

Hospital Sunday, Sway, 29 June 1924. The procession is approaching the railway bridge in Station Road. The Forest Heath Hotel is behind the trees on the left.

Fawley Village, *c.* 1905. In 1863 John Wise describes the road from Hythe to Calshot: 'True English lanes will lead us by quiet dells, with glimpses here and there through hedgerow elms of the blue Southampton water, down to the shore of the Solent'. Transformation of the area began in 1920 with the building of the AGWI (later Esso) oil refinery.

Near Copthorne House, Fawley, *c.* 1930. Copthorne House was lived in by Captain Cecil Drummond (1890), Samuel Montgomerie JP at the turn of the twentieth century and, in the 1930s, by Henry Demoulins.

Burley village, *c.* 1890. The centre of Burley village showing the gate and tree, left foreground, of the Tree House.

The Burley Midget charabanc, *c.* 1922. It ran twice a week to Bournemouth and once a week to Southampton and Ringwood market. It could also be hired for private functions. The owner was Alan Taylor, shown here in the driver's seat, and it was driven by Reg Boyall.

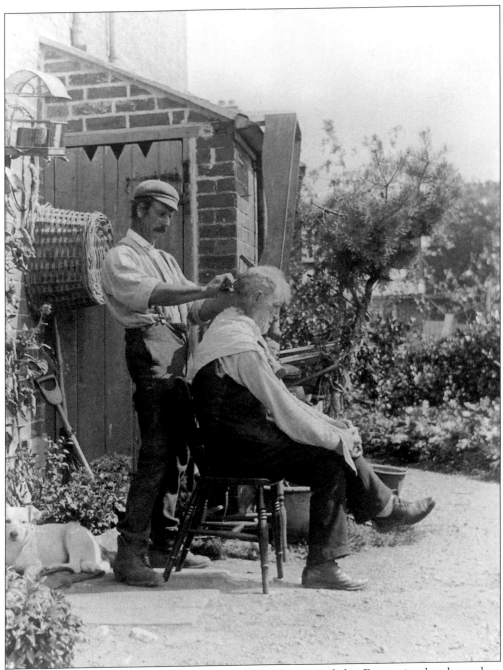

Village haircutting, New Forest. In the outlying districts of the Forest, in the days when transport was limited, an itinerant barber, who often combined his trade with tooth-pulling, could expect to make a reasonable living by offering his services *in situ*.

The Fleur de Lys pub at Pilley, *c.* 1914. Two customers enjoy a pint outside the village pub. The publican at this time was Alfred Pearce. The Fleur de Lys is mentioned in the Revd Comyn's notebooks a century before (1817) as an alehouse run by John Youngs and his two nieces Mary and Anne.

Furzey Cottage, South Weirs, Brockenhurst, *c.* 1950. To the south-west of Brockenhurst village lie North and South Weirs, a few scattered houses on either side of a drainage channel dug by the Forestry Commission. Folk from the Weirs were once known by the Brockenhurst villagers as 'rough and wild'.

Cottages on 'Hare and Hounds' Hill, Durns Town, Sway, *c.* 1905. Mrs Rose Rickman is taking her baby for a stroll.

Women's Cricket Team, Beaulieu, *c.* 1910. Three of the players are Muriel, Sybil and Diana Biddlecombe, daughters of Samuel Biddlecombe of Swinesley's Farm, Beaulieu.

Visiting performing bear, New Forest. For Forest children, unused to being entertained, the bear must have caused great excitement.

New Forest Refreshment Rooms, High Street, Lyndhurst, *c.* 1915. From left to right: F.W. Howard by the cycle, Mrs Bull with two children in the doorway, Mr Bull, and Mr King. Today there is a camping shop on this site.

Post Office Workers, Lyndhurst, 1915. Second left in the back row is Miss Alice Macey who lived in the High Street, Lyndhurst into her old age.

Church parade, Beaulieu Camp, 1909. E. Stevens, a photographer from Poole, issued a series of images featuring the military camp at Beaulieu.

Fritham, c. 1905. Fritham, in the north, is one of the most isolated communities in the Forest, surrounded by heath and ancient woodland.

Before the First World War, and in some areas until the 1930s, milk was delivered to customers in cans that were filled from a churn transported in a pony cart. The milk was dipped out with a long handled measure. This photograph is thought to be of Mr Penny, from Blackwater Farm, Emery Down on his milk round around 1920.

Life-long Commoner Mr Harry Burt outside his Brockenhurst smallholding, *c.* 1950.

Walden's shop at Norleywood, *c.* 1910. This was a branch of Shelley's grocery store at Pilley. Most village shops operated from commandeered cottage sitting rooms.

The local infants decked out in their finery for the Brockenhurst Prize Babies competition, around 1920.

The Meadow End Light Railway, *c.* 1965. The model railway at Brockenhurst operated for several years raising money for charity, often the International League for the Protection of Horses. The train driver is Mark Abbott.

Seven
Fighting the Elements

Snow at Stoney Cross, *c.* 1937. This photograph was used as an advertisement for Bluecol anti-freeze. It was a good choice of subject as Stoney Cross is one of the bleakest and most exposed areas of the Forest.

The centre of Burley village, *c.* 1960. The summer 'honey-pot' as few visitors see it. The garage on the left is now, like most premises in Burley, a gift shop.

St Nicholas church, Brockenhurst lays claim to being the oldest church in the Forest as it is mentioned in *Domesday Book*. Evidence of late Norman architecture can be seen in the south doorway and inside is a lead-lined font, made of Purbeck stone, dating from the twelfth century.

The Watersplash, Brockenhurst, frozen over, probably in the hard winter of 1962/63.

Flood Waters. The hardy New Forest pony is used to coping with all that nature can devise.

Lyndhurst Road, Brockenhurst, in flood, 1958/59. Low-lying Brockenhurst is particularly vulnerable in times of heavy rainfall.

Waters Green Road, 3 February 1990. The 'Little Watersplash', as it is known to locals, is overwhelmed and two residents, Millie Ferret and Anne Cobb, help one another across.

Lyndhurst church struck by lightning on 16 March 1913. This photograph shows the damage to the base of the tower.

The damaged west doorway after the lightning strike, Lyndhurst church, 1913.

Fire at Littlecroft, Emery Down, 2 August 1913. Littlecroft was the home of Morton Kelsall Peto, whose father Samuel was the contractor who built the Southampton to Dorchester railway line. Morton was an artist who exhibited in London in the 1880s. The only part of the house that was not damaged in the fire was his studio. Most of the furniture was rescued and can be seen stacked in the garden.

Cadland Farm Fire, 11 March 1923. This scene was captured by Edward Mudge whose photographic studio was on the first floor of Ashlett Mill.

Honeysuckle Tea Cottage, Minstead as it appeared in 1950. Probably built in the late 1920s the house, with its quaint thatch, seemed older.

Honeysuckle tea rooms and restaurant, Minstead, alight, 18 March 1999. The fire was presumed to have begun when a spark from a garden bonfire caught the thatch. Although firemen worked tirelessly for several hours, the building was gutted. More than two years later it is still a burnt-out shell.

Brockenhurst fire brigade, 5 July 1932, showing the brigade and Crossley fire engine outside the fire station in Fibbards Road. From left to right, bottom row: N. Holtom, W. Hayward, W. Hiett (captain), J.R. Stevens (second officer), J.W. Martin (secretary), F. Field (foreman), A. Plumbly, C. Gill, J. Dunkinson. Second row: E. Pascoe, F. Marden (station engineer), I. Lee, G. Blackwell, H. Bowden, and E. Stride. Third row: E. Purse, and C. Pink.

Brockenhurst fire brigade. This photograph was taken on 23 January 1934 when fireman Fred Marden (right) left the brigade and handed over the duties of driver/mechanic to fireman Cliff Gulliver. Shown is the Crossley fire engine and the new Pulsometer trailer pump.

Eight

The Borders

Ringwood Market Place, c. 1920. Ringwood was given a charter to sell agricultural animals and produce in 1266 and it is believed that cattle, and other stock, were sold here continuously until the final market was held on 29 June 1988. The light fitting was erected by subscription in 1887 to commemorate the Golden Jubilee of the reign of Queen Victoria.

The Old Cottage tea rooms, Ringwood, *c.* 1920. The Elizabethan Cottages still operate as a restaurant.

THE NEW FOREST.

When
in the New
Forest call at

The Old Cottage Tea Rooms

(adjoining the Historical Monmouth House)

Ringwood.

⊕

Teas served in the quaint old rooms
or in the garden by the River Avon.

⊕

Luncheons.   Dainty Teas.
Home made Cakes and Scones.
Parties Catered for.

⊕

Do not fail to see these Picturesque
Elizabethan Cottages.

An advert for The Old Cottage tea rooms, Ringwood, which appeared in Heywood Sumner's *Guide to the New Forest* around the time the above photograph was taken.

Monmouth House, Ringwood. Following his defeat at the Battle of Sedgemoor in 1685, the Duke of Monmouth, having been captured nearby, was held in this house prior to his execution in the Tower of London. The house is next to the Old Cottage Restaurant and close to the River Avon.

Opposite Monmouth House today is the Armfield Technical Education building. The advert above, from around 1925, shows that an earlier incarnation of the Armfield organization were experts in a different field.

RINGWOOD.

On the Border of the New Forest.

It is here that one of the largest industries of its kind in this Country can be found, viz. : the manufacture of

WATER TURBINES

the most up-to-date means of obtaining Power from Water for Driving

Electric Light Installations

Estate and Saw Mill Machinery, Pumps for Towns Water Supply, and all kinds of Machinery where **Water Power** is available.

Apply for fully illustrated Catalogue from the Manufacturers :

Joseph J. Armfield & Co., Ltd.,
Hydraulic Engineers.

Southampton Street, Ringwood, *c.* 1910. The post office, on the left, is now a job centre. The postmaster at the turn of the twentieth century was George Lee Pearce Polden.

Lymington High Street, *c.* 1900, looking east towards The Quay. The proprietor of the Angel Hotel, on the left, at this time was John Walter. The hotel also acted as the headquarters for the cycle and cricket clubs.

Lymington High Street, looking west towards St Thomas's church, *c.* 1900. The parish church, which has medieval origins, is very attractive with a distinctive cupola on the west tower, probably built in the eighteenth century. The vicar in 1900 was the Revd Benjamin Maturin.

Boats at anchor, Lymington River, *c.* 1900. The coastal area of Lymington was once renowned for its salt works, with salt-houses and salterns extending along the coast from Pylewell to Hurst. The last saltern remained in use until 1865.

Air Training Corps, Lymington, 1942. From left to right, back row: Sgt Clive 'Curly' Lewington, -?-, Perriton, -?-, -?-, Harold Hendey, -?-, -?-. Centre row: -?-, Frank Webb, -?-. Front row (sitting): David Jones, -?-, -?-, -?-. Clive Lewington was killed in a plane crash in the Far East in 1945.

Passford Farm, near Lymington, *c.* 1890. Passford Farm was once part of the St Austin's Estate owned by the Bishop of Lincoln. The farmhouse was severely damaged by fire in December 1992.

St Thomas Street, Lymington, *c.* 1900. The Dorset Arms, on the right, was run at this time by Henry Edmonds.

An aerial view of Sway showing Lunns Sawmills (centre foreground). Lunns was one of the major timber producers in the south of England. It was destroyed by fire on 22 November 1963, the same day that US President John F. Kennedy was assassinated.

Peterson's Tower, Sway, c. 1905. This solid concrete edifice was built in 1879/84 by Judge Andrew Peterson who had amassed a fortune as a barrister in defending Indian Princes and Nabobs for their part in the massacres of Delhi, Lucknow etc., during the Indian Mutiny of 1857. It is said by some to have been erected solely to give work to a number of unemployed men in the locality; and by others, simply to extol the virtues of concrete. Not surprisingly, perhaps, it is also known as Peterson's Folly.

The road to Nomansland, *c.* 1940. Standing on the edge of the New Forest and on the Hampshire/Wiltshire border, Nomansland is a tiny hamlet, set around a village green, with close links to nearby Bramshaw.

Cottage Homes, Nomansland, *c.* 1905. New Forest cob cottages were built of clay mixed with straw or chopped heather. H.M. Livens, writing in 1910, describes the building process and says of the Nomansland cottages: '...thus carefully built, thatched and whitewashed, a mud cottage with walls from eighteen inches to two feet thick, was more snug and waterproof than an ordinary brick one, besides costing far less to erect, and looking much more comely in the end.'

Coronation street party, Rushington, 1953. Rushington Manor, to the west of Totton, was once a large estate (220 acres which included Testbourne House) owned latterly by the Birch-Reynardson family. The estate's home farm was on Rushington Lane. Anciently, the Manor of Rushington (or Rumbridge) was owned by the Crown and in 1159 was granted to Cobb the Smith who provided barbed arrows for the king when he rode out to hunt in the Forest.

Dibden church, c. 1910. All Saints was the first church in Britain to be damaged by enemy action in the Second World War. Much damage was sustained and many treasures lost but it was restored and rebuilt by 1955. Nearby Dibden Purlieu, owes its name to its earlier associations with the Forest. 'Purlieu' means a tract of land formerly in the forest.

Moyles Court, near Ringwood, c. 1910. Moyles Court was once home to Alice Lisle (c. 1614 - 1685) who was famously condemned to be beheaded by Judge Jeffreys for sheltering two anti-royalist supporters on their flight during the Monmouth rebellion. Moyles Court is now a private school.

A Motor Car ✍ ✍ ✍

is the finest possible medium whereby
Tourists can view the sublime scenery

in The New Forest.

THOROUGHLY
RELIABLE
CARS
FOR
HIRE
BY
THE
HOUR,
DAY,
OR
WEEK

12 H.P. WOLSELEY CAR.

TRAINS
OR
BOATS
MET
UPON
RECEIPT
OF
LETTER,
TELEGRAM,
OR ORDER
BY 'PHONE.

**The sense of power, speed and safety of the motor, combined
with the magnificent splendour of the scenery, indelibly impress
themselves upon the memory, making the drive
a never-to-be-forgotten event.**

*We have splendidly appointed Cars for hire, and driven by experienced chauffeurs.
Terms upon application.*

F. A. HENDY & CO., LTD.,

MOTOR AND CYCLE ENGINEERS,

EAST STREET, SOUTHAMPTON.

Telegrams :—HENDY, SOUTHAMPTON.   Telephone :—461 SOUTHAMPTON.

This advert appeared in Mate's *Illustrated Guide to Hampshire and the Isle of Wight* in 1905.

A New Forest log team in the late 1940s.

Acknowledgments

My grateful thanks to the New Forest Ninth Centenary Trust, Lyndhurst who gave me exceptional access to their photographic archive while compiling this book. My special thanks to the Chief Librarian Jude James, whose help was invaluable, the Deputy Librarian Richard Reeves and Peter Roberts who joined me so enthusiastically in the research, provided photographs and willingly shared his extensive local knowledge. I would also like to acknowledge my debt to Judith Warbey, Diana Daniell, Barry Peckham, Jenny Plucknett and Rosemary Manning. Some of the material used from the New Forest Ninth Centenary Trust was courtesy of Noel Grover.